Loss of Others

by

J. D. Stewart

Copyright © 2013
ISBN-13: 978-1490553191
ISBN-10: 1490553193

To Barbara who has committed to teaching me civility.

Man is by nature a political animal; and so even when men have no need of assistance from each other they none the less desire to be together. At the same time, they are also brought together by common interest, so far as each achieves a share of the good life. The good life then is the chief aim or the political community, both collectively and individually.

Aristotle, *Politics*

Preface

I have long wondered what caused a decrease in the geniality and camaraderie that once graced interaction among Americans. The desire to win, identification of self as a victim or interpersonal animosity even within families seems epidemic. The loss of care for others, which I had known in my childhood, is no longer fashionable and has been replaced by an abject, self-consuming insularity.

What is happening to replace the valued affability of the individual, the love of one's neighbor? It would be comforting to think that this is just a secondary loss of favor with others, that other perturbations in a much faster lifestyle had brought about this cooling of care-fulness. But if this argument is pursued it will point to deeper concerns; it is more complex and involved than merely being swamped by the expectations of a demanding lifestyle. We have primarily lost the love of neighbor in part and as a result of losing the love of ourselves as an extension of the others and is even marked by a substantial dissolution of even unavoidable associations. Not that we don't want for ourselves all that is good, it is that we have compromised the very receptivity that would allow us to appreciate self-reward putting all our efforts in self-satisfaction. We have become complete in our solipsistic tendencies and have convinced ourselves that we can be fulfilled with mere self-containment. We have lost the genuine ability to respond to the needs of others. We have lost what it means to be human. We have lost humane identity.

I fear for a people that looses its greatness for the hope of finding completion in self. This could possibly be referent to what has been attributed to Alexis de Tocqueville, that is, that the loss of America's goodness would result in the default of its greatness. Why is goodness, that personal relational quality of humans, of key importance? The object of goodness must be directed toward the outer, the other, not the in-animation of each life but the invigoration and care of others. Recent denials of interpersonal responsibility have driven me to this project. How does a life spin only in its own orbit and fail to truly find the meaningful gravitas of true interactive attachment to others. What does it mean to have friendships realized in our daily life apart from special occasions where nominal community imposes itself?

If we have no deep concern for others, what will be the fall out? And if we avoid them, how will that effect them? What are we missing and what are we denying others in our abandonment? This may sound like the concern is referent to the hermitic life that lives unto self alone, but in reality that is practically impossible today. The lack of community is not solved by the family which Tocqueville clearly saw as purely individualistic and self-serving, denying in effect all others and finding a self justification in caring exclusively for familial others as an extension of themselves. We share our own with others as a validation of our otherness, only to care little about the recipients who are only necessary to record the existence of an almost patrician singularity. There is a subtlety in consideration of what Tocqueville may have had in mind. A superficiality may show the extent of the inclination to self and selfness. The Christmas card is a picture of such centeredness consisting of the family with words that do not represent the seasonal wishes but the evidence of superlative breeding and pride of ownership. The invitation to dine may be merely self-aggrandizement that challenges those in attendance to pick up the gauntlet.

Alice's adventures, which are depicted at the beginning of each chapter, the Introduction and the Conclusion, may be seen as one trying to skirt authority in rebellion against others. Alice may have wanted a world in which she could do as she wished without the control of others, but there is a way to see her actions as more dismissive of others than merely willfully self-assertive. Many of these John Tenniel illustrations suggest a pouty immaturity that is in keeping with a modern view of failure, to not attain one's self rights. Apart from the real world which did not accept her on her own terms, she found her own authority and expressed her wishes in a world in which she had no deeply concerned citizenship. If we were to be honest with ourselves, most of us elect to have little integral involvement in the world around us as we pick and choose what we want to attend to and then ignore most everything else. As individuals we do not always seem well grounded or balanced in a world which changes so rapidly, but, without complete acceptance of the world around us, we still willfully lavish on ourselves the justification that would deny the right of personal authority and goodwill to others. We have denied their right to be considered favorably. This book is about what has been lost in our sacrifice of the recognition of others, what we have lost in the superficial, the mundane, and the deep considerations of community and how we might understand the loss so as to reclaim others and ourselves once again.

Lewis Caroll gave the world Alice and her adventures, but the genius of John Tenniel gave us a view of that world in amazing illustrations. It is my privilege to humbly draw on several of his ninety or more drawings which he provided Carrol for the two Alice books, *Alice's Adventures in Wonderland (1865)* and *Through the Looking-Glass And What Alice Found There (1871)*. The hope is that the illustrations that appear here along with The Child Alone illustration from *A Child's Garden of Verses* by Robert Louis Stevenson (1905) will add a degree of visual delight to the text. Again it is a privilege to see these drawings, from public domain in the United States of America, find their way before a new generation of readers a century and a half after they were first published.

J. D. Stewart

May 25, 2013

The Mad Hatter and the March
Hare rudely dunk the Dormouse
in the teapot.

Table of Contents

Introduction

One of the great mysteries of mankind is how we can grown and develop while retaining what we are: that which identifies us as ourselves. People who, upon meeting one another after years of separation, find not only recognizability in one another but can often without awkward pleasantries immediately take up where their previous relationships left off as if no time was lost in their friendship. There is something special in that reunion; it is not merely knowledge of the persons reunited, but an organic kinship in which all parties may find extreme value, for self and others, far beyond nostalgic remembrance. There is in the meeting, a sense of finding oneself in some associative form. One grows from pre-established development from a past and precedes through a rekindling of growth to a progressive renewal of self. This self is nurtured by the contact with formative others, the remembrance that carries with it the recognition of the other and strangely the recognition of self through the re-association. This experience, says that the other person is important in defining self, of giving meaning, personality and solidity to becoming an independent person. That person then becomes the interactive force in the lives of others to enrich and to grow us into more fully sentient creatures.

Temporary re-association, for example, at Christmas or a class reunion may allow us to recapture some of the caring from the past. But day to day what relational attitudes do we present among others? What is the effect when this mutually conducive development is interfered with by a severing of real relationships among family and immediate friends in the long term? It is interesting that the killing of a single bee may herald a hive war against the killer. There is a chemical connection between apiary members, one that is a common connection among that community. Do humans have any of this, have we ever? And if we have had a strong connectivity, maybe not chemical or mechanical, but, if so, is it still strong enough to draw us to the care and defense of relationships with the other ? A boy finds a girl and the "chemistry" is real. Perhaps this is the beginning of an attraction that is greater than some pheromonal mechanism. Apart from such strong desires for intimacy among true lovers, is it possible that we, in ordinary daily associations, tend to less meaningful and mutually supportive associations with others which are not so intimately bound to our lives?

I believe that the running commentary among citizens of modern America is based on a distrust and selfishness that imbues every area of normal daily life. The people with which we work, the motorist on the street with us, the governmental official we are bound to elect, all have lost out on the respect and consideration that once may have been accorded them. It would seem that we are in competition with everyone for every emotional and material possibility for success. To allow others to have what we have or want is to not be able to have the same thing as there is a limited supply of success with happiness thus being restricted in the lack. There is the demonstration of untoward anger and aggressiveness that results in further distancing one from another. The loss of civility and general concern for others has given even passing relationships and loose associations with others a sense of dread for anyone who would see kindness a commodity easily dispensed to those of close or even distant associations. There is a sense in which we can by our very neglect or animosity toward others elicit a ragging torrent of ill feelings or insouciance in dropping others from our radar and, in effect, failing to acknowledge their existence. This is possibly what Alice had in mind when she went through the looking glass into a world that she wished to control and from which she could find separation from the presence and authority of others.

Rene Descartes, a seventeenth century philosopher and mathematician gave us the doubt of the presence of others. In fact he doubted his very existence and the world around him, and only through his rationalistic attempt to demonstrate his consideration of the power of thought did he concede that there was indeed a world in which his mental activity was at play. This was a watershed speculation that has implication today in our consideration of others. Certainly in a practical exploration of this idea, to imagine that we are the center of the universe is, in a sense, dependent on those undeniable perceptions of the world around us, our immediate world. Our focus on self, could come to be seen as, if not merely controlled or serendipitous illusions, then unimportant animations in an ego-centrist world. The lack of importance of others is heavily reinforced in our actions and attitudes by the appeals that are constantly made to individual wants and desires, the focus on the freedom and autonomy of each of us through a modern understanding infused in advertising, entertainment, culture and family by tacit directives that by synecdoche, in the name of personal freedom, misrepresents individual importance. When our understanding of the world results in our seeing others as merely means to our own ends or as obstacles to our own wills, then we enter through our own lives into a sort of Cartesian mirror of skepticism, that is destructive to community and even to ourselves. In the process we only create an illusory world of self-importance by denying the inter-relatedness of all humanity.

I have known only a few people that seem to be immune to the presence and needs of others at any level. These sad people seemed incapable of sympathy, necessarily empathy, and lived as if they were the only reason for all existence. They were not obviously malicious and were even quite well liked by those who mixed with them casually. True solipsism is rare, if not impossible, but solitary individuals, as far I have been able to determine, seem to believe that they are characteristic of the species, that nothing about them is substantially different from any other of their kind. There is, therefore, no reason for carefully socializing with others for to do so would only be a lesser approximation of self-aggrandizement. If there is any truth in this observation, then are we seeing a new modification or adaptation to man who was for eons at least a functional, if not a caring, communal animal ? If this is a true adaptation, then is it being propagated among us by and to the exclusion of even an idea of community ? If this condition is growing among us can we do something to reverse the tendency, or are we to expect to see man inculcated by the rage of self ?

Perhaps this is mere fanciful speculation and we are as we always have been, but we are more prone to the immediate doing in our lives today and have little time or thought for those that might require from us as we are the observers of need, but we have not connected sufficiently such that we can feel the real needs of others. Government often attends to need blindly, never seeing the needy, indeed never consistently seeing the real need. Feeling is so rampant today that among our citizenry there could be a collective desensitization to real need. Let the government or other institutions handle the need. The end result of such behavior may result in reason possibly consuming reasonable caring, for we tend to hold more trust in feelings than by reason or evidence. So depending on the connection between the two understandings, if linked, we may have fatally compromised the authentic reading of feeling and emotion. Most of us can find a tear welling up in sentimental movies as we are manipulated by the entertainment formula. We have the simulacrum of emotionality, but do we truly have the ability to perform sensitively, to be truly moved by emotional issues and situations? Do we truly care about others ? The most important and most bewildering question is: Why do we need to understand and reach out to those who are around us everyday? To make some progress in this enigmatic ignor-ance of the other, we must examine a relationship that is troubling and one that is mechanically disregarded by most of us at least some of the time.

Chapter 1

Others

A child may look to mother and father for care and love getting what is needed with a cry or a smile. A child is totally dependent and yet gives as gets. The parents are enthralled with this infusion of personality and joy, and most will sacrifice most any thing for this legacy. Most children open to others as they grow as an outgrowth of the love and nurture given them as babes. Most parents are concerned about their children, maybe even more concerned about those dangers that seem in more recent times to have found children an object of abuse. We begin our introit into decision making being told not to talk to strangers or even to venture out of parents' sight. Although a serious proposition today, it is as it has always been: parents want to protect their children from all danger.

So we begin our freedom of responses as leery inexperienced babes, unable to make good decisions and being told that there are dangers out there for which we are to be cautious. Betrayal has inauspicious beginnings as a product of unguarded naiveté. A friend takes a toy and we learn to horde toys and prevent others from playing with them. Having and keeping for oneself becomes a general practice and suspicion grows with the value of the objects envied by others. Or maybe we are progressively self-programmed to withdrawn our courtesy to others as it conflicts with our own desires and selfishness. Each of these considerations, abuse, being taken advantage for our possessions and even natural tendencies, point to an early and progressive distancing of us and ours from others outside of our guaranteed trust.

But there is no denying that adults find identification through interaction with others. *Homosapien*, wise man, could just as well be *homocommunitas*, man gifted with the spirit of togetherness, for as it has been suggested by centuries of communal life, man seems to be drawn to live among others of his own kind. Whether that interaction is enforced by social or business associations, as we mature we must be exposed to others, yet we do not have to give our trust only our interactivity, in near proximity. It may be to our mutual benefit that we join in activities. There may be, at the same time, somewhat of a discontent and distrust from which we withdraw when we can. The evolution of associations, as opposed to meaningful relationships with others, will be recognized and valued as a way to advance oneself. The rationale is that one's environment improves as a function of group purpose, so does each members expectations for success and getting what each member wants. We may indulge others for that leg up on success we are seeking as a variety of appealing advantages are offered by the group extending the benefits of our own limited contribution. We can ride the coattails of others as they can ride ours. There is no misunderstanding, we need them and they may need us. Our collective bounty may be reaped together but what we want is singularly for self.

Dependence on others marks the divide among members of the group. Shared success may mean a reduced status for each member. The capability of fellow workers making the desired impression or doing the specialty work that a project requires may diminish the self valuing of the individual, but perhaps the worst of all reductionist effects is that by our work we are known only in association with others and in a narrower specialized contribution.

We become identified with others, whether we like it or not. Only partially identified in the organic makeup of the group, we are dependent on others to identify us. We must depend on others for a great part of our identity. Yet division of labor and personal variety distracts from recognition. The idea that everyone that we meet would look, act and have the same desires and tastes is rather boring and being loss in homogeneity would further assert our contributing value as little more than drones. But variety is but the spice that, at the same time, takes a slice of our persona.

The other represents what we are not in alternate parts or in variation. It identifies us as possibly worthy, by contrast, but may find by comparison to others that we are in some manner lacking. We may dismiss others as Alice did in labeling them only a "pack of cards." We bear different markings to identify us but we are virtually the same, two-dimensional and non-consequential.

We may raise our self-opinion by looking to those considered less successful, talented or attractive, yet we are to be haunted by the existence of others that are grander than ourselves in as many ways as those that we value. In addition those that we look down on may be better than we think, as those we look up to. We may even feel loss from the shear dilution by others among whom we seek recognition. In a since this envy and derision may give us the depths to which we should not fall and may spark us to push ourselves beyond the heights to which we wish to reach. In essence, we have a gauge of expectations, limitations that define who we are, who we think we are and how far we believe we may progress. The others represent the hope that we have for rising in our own eyes and gaining the prideful recognition of others. Those at the top of our expectations, those that we would strive to be like or even directly replicate in ability and positive recognition by others, become our models. They become our heroes in a sense. This does not mean that we even like them. They are a working standard that we will chase in our activities in order to attain that image or ability to which we have dedicated our efforts.

Although we originate our persona, we are, after all, acting in response to our upbringing and our changing environment. It is not a new thought but an unavoidable one: we are to some extent actors. We read our parts in life under the sway of family, the perspective of uniqueness and self-preservation. That which is not scripted by our surroundings and upbringing is ad libbed, one would hope, with the sensitivity and appropriateness commensurate with the situation. Meeting obstacles in life requires the application of innovation, but the way that we greet the new may reflect frustration, anger or even joy. The last possibility seems fleeting in a world in which many will get what is desired with little or no consideration of others. It is easily said that the others are those that do not have our best interests at the heart of their desires. The truth is that for many the desires of the others may not even register with us. The others in more recent times have become lost in our concern and often in our fleeting consideration. They are there. They will not go away. If we were to seriously consider the world without others, we would be challenged to find good reason to carry on, yet often we act in their presence as if they were the ruination of a good world, our world. If this is fallacious reasoning unfair to both ourselves and others, then there needs to be a restoration of contact, consideration and faith in the necessity and respect for others. To put it in more direct relationship: we are the other to others.

The banking fiasco, investment scams, denial that debt is an option, these are all manifestations of the loss of others. The best reason to become concerned with others if not for our own view of ourselves is to provide a just treatment which we would judge fair if our lives and livelihood were in jeopardy.

Chapter 2

What do we want for them ?

"Off with her head !"

An understanding of others is not always considered in optimistic communitarian terms. Gustave Le Bon, in his book entitled *The Crowd*, found little to recommend the group, the assembly with others (The Crowd: A Study of the Popular Mind, NY, 1896). His view of groups was that they constituted a mob, which was as a group unintelligent, emotionally unstable and potentially violent and for which nothing constructive could have ever been originary due to a dilution of reasoned members, by sheer numbers of those unable to make rational decisions. He further believed that no great idea of reason, business or government has ever been blessed by a large cooperative in intelligent creativity except first given direction by an elitist cabal or aristocracy which dictated the path of action to thus enslave the masses. This was admittedly severely written by one who saw no benefit in decisions being determined by mass action. By fiat the Queen would have the head of every recalcitrant and malingerer. It would seem that Le Bon would favor such a decisive governance, a monarchy over an exclusively open democracy without the Queen's personalized command of the law of execution. But to take his understanding of initiative on the part of the few, as the guiding principles on which masses but follow, the group becomes the mind and influence of the individual.

It is the good and the bad that we receive from those that we look to for leadership and friendship. Le Bon sees that there are degrees of association with others, and it is true that he saw larger groups being more problematic to relationships and intellectual integrity. Although written in the early nineteenth century Tocqueville's penetrating understanding of American individualism, which he described in *Democracy in America,* is, I believe, even more pertinent today. Groups with which we have intimate associations, such as relatives, are so close that these relationships may fall under the umbrella designation of individualism in the larger context. This distinctly close type of America affiliation is not extensively the meaning that is given here for the "Other." The intension is to consider our relationships not to mobs or our essentially extended family but to those we interact with in what may be more perfunctory associations. Many of these people we see as having little to no impact on our lives, while others are influencing us and effecting us for good or, as we may see it, for bad.

We are indebted to those that provide us with advantages. These may be bosses, parents, friends or business associates that manage to give our lives and careers new turns and opportunities. We want to nurse their attention until it over steps those personal boundaries which we guard, those barriers to our closest selves. Usually our parents are removed from the ultimate decision-making process much later than either we or they would like. Our boss either is unwelcome inside the fortress of our self-defining natures or is forced to only enter the atrium, where all may inquire within. We then prevent the entrance into the definitive areas of our lives that maintain and extend the separation of others from our own identity-forming activities and persona. Our friends may find a well-delineated space in our lives with little carryover to other areas and serve as a reserve option for times when something like friendship is needed as in times of trouble or grief.

Wanting what others have to give does not mean that we can control the intrusiveness of their involvement in our lives. Bosses controlling our personal life is expected to some extent, after all that is why we are paid, but the separation of our physical presence from the job site does not mean that we are capable of separating our mental domain from the imposition of work issues. Superiors are the unavoidable prime providers of our lifestyle and possibly much about how we think, but we provide the work that justifies their jobs and the interests that employs both the managers and their workers. Our work becomes a justification of ourselves by properly disposing of the business which we are assigned. We trade the security of rank in order to optimize business associations.

We have a bond in family that is of ourselves in part and by nature a more custodial relationship often mediated by grandchildren. A legacy of concerns that to the son or daughter, mother or fathers is autotelic often stretching no further than one's concern for self. Although parents give us life and nurture, they are unable to be comfortably separated from us and seem to intermingle with us in physical similarities and personality traits. Individuals from generations apart begin to run together among other family members such that one family member may stand in synecdoche for family traits without reduction or blurring of mutual recognition to membership in the clan. The result is looking at parents as we get older and seeing ourselves. No doubt there is jealousy in seeing the former authorities in our lives reading, directing and advising us and leaving a sense of reduced self-control over our lives.

When speaking of the true others, not in the immediate familiar sphere, we must acknowledge that for some that we know we are dependent as adults and work and find security in them as providers. They are our introit into the work and social world. They give us recognition and share their measured celebrity at the possible cost of their own social currency. When they take us on as friends or partners in the work force, say, we then offer others our potential for improving their lot or we may, by taking a chance, be found to compromise the offer of our help or our friendship.

We may feel that we are being told what to want by those who most probably do not know us and are not concerned about our welfare. Yet the vivid and detached luminaries of screen and song, are often the occupation of our minds and emotions. These celebrity images and sound bites, make overtures to others for the others become the desired cash nexus and those who could extend a brief season of adulation. We are the dollar signs in their eyes and, admittedly, as fickle as their admirers in their season. We scream, defy and alienate those whom we have real life experience, fleshly associations, and yet, ironically, we defer to those idols and kings of our desires. We usurp the normal growth of

responsible ideation, and, by not striving for objective or even caringly emotive understanding, we disregard the value of positively weighing associations and interpersonal issues. We pigeonhole everyone; it makes life so much easier to avoid by seeing collective and limited characteristics rather than individual character. And finally we cannot be moved to deep kindness and understanding since that is only achieved by empathetic concern for an individual's plight. We generally hold others as semiotic antitheses to the real as those who would be for us just as human if they were without breath and pulse. Do we want to take fame for our anonymity, a bit of élan for our entropic energies ? We want the notable others to be less than us, to be incomparable to our shining. We want what they are. We will be mean and demean others to get it. Despite the fact that by co-opting others we can only absorb a fleeting association with fame, we adopt the look, the close and the habits of
our alter-egos.

Although we may eschew the common others and despite this disdain we want the very object of our derision, the non-famed others, to be our audience. To hear our discontent with ourselves, railing against our failures, this is the most often maladjusted use of others, the means or our own ends. The ability to rile others as we verbally attack is a sign that we are ourselves with greater power than they. We measure our power by the reduced authority of others.

It is interesting that so often today protest is unsure of its purpose. It stands in the face of what is thought of as abused authority and renounces those abuses. But we are really saying that we have less power and want more. The only problem is that we do not always know how we were to apply such power had we a bit of it and when we would need to stop in our pursuit of it. Le Bon saw that once a person moves to the fore, there is little stopping leadership except limits and direction. He feels, and perhaps rightly so, that leaders merely follow and often create little real direction for the crowd and their demands but merely echo the shouts. The leader becomes the one that as a single voice can scream the demands that each crowd member would want heard. We want to be recognized and to succeed on that recognition to a state of authority above others.

Chapter 3

What should they be able to expect from us ?

Those in need want help from us whether we are their friends or they are merely the unnamed needy. Can we deny them aid ? If we don't help them, what does that say about us ? But, if we help them, do we condescend to give them food and shelter ? Some believe that only the government can help the needy without there being a inadvertent elevation of the helpers' egos and resultant condescension to the needy. To ignore the personal need of others without being moved to personally help, seems a self-condemnation of coldness. It is easier to let some agency do the helping. That way we don't get our hands dirty. Do we owe others our personal time and energy as well as a handout ? If, on the other hand, we let an impersonal agency help the needy, then we are free to live our lives without direct concern by merely paying the money for their needs. Certainly for both the needy and ourselves we must be inconvenienced and to share in the personal recognition and involvement with those that need help. Without helping we come to close the door a little bit more on our insular lives in which all of our thoughts are about ourselves, more self-sufficient and yet even about those we might emulate, those that have everything they want and need, and yet want more.

That is not to say that there are people who could, but will not, do for themselves and that to care for them when they are unwilling to care for themselves only turns into a handout that will very well be squandered. As far as our own view of the aiding of those who have no higher expectations for themselves, we are made to look at waste in the personification of the ungrateful. This said, we are better off erring on the side of the foolish than to withhold that for which someone has need. We must take the chance that we will be made to look like fools in hopes that someone who we help may be refreshed and stirred to an appreciation of the help offered. The those that are needed should be able to count on our help to give them the benefit of the doubt about their deserving aid. In fact, such a gesture of giving that recognizes the needs of others also recognizes the worth of another human life with valuation beyond a mere handout.

The ultimate justification for our being found duped and made fools of is that our motivation was sincere and merely the result of offering aid to those believed to be in need. If this is wrong, sorry. If being made to appear a fool and the brunt of a shameful scam, then we must live with it. Ours is not to know all people, their motivation and designs, it is only for us to venture hope and extend services to others ostensibly in need. Let us be made fools for the potential of helping others. This is what should be expected of us. Why should we leave such care to the bureaucrats who have doubtful real contact with the needy, even to the extent that the real needs may not be understood and inappropriate "aid" be given. The risk is that the receipt may be seen as an entitlement for which it may be difficult for the recipient to latter reject. Let us as individuals become a sacrifice for the presumed needy.

The issue of alms for the needy is much more easily dealt with than the sacrificial giving of ourselves to others because we value them as human beings. Apart from materials needs those around us need the offering of our time, attention and ultimately our concern for their well-being. How difficult it is for us to tear ourselves away from the plenty we may enjoy to give to those who are not suffering from material deficiency. This idea of sacrificing the time and concern that costs us nothing but costs us our very affluent moments is so strange, so foreign to us today, that a moment of anger at a motorist is not followed by any thought of the possibility that that person may be experiencing a deep regret or need, not in possessions, but in emotional or spiritual need. How close life has come to solipsism at this moment, a moment to be quickly forgotten, yet one that is in part the mortar that may help bind the stones of our isolation. As the wall is formed one experiential stone at a time we become more and more convinced that we are justified and others are less and less worthy of the disdain we feel for those who do not consider our wills and wishes above their own.

This perfusion of exclusionary self-interest in to all areas of life, I believe, through a modern world of success-oriented individualism, has left us insensate to the lives of others not intimately associated with us. This precludes community and country leaving each of us to get what we can, if, in the process, we deny others their right to not only have a good life but to be recognized as worthy of such a life.

Chapter 4

What emerging attitudes arise from self ?

Modern childhood gropes for a sense of self by pressing parents to release power which the child applies to a expanding world through manipulative control. This is the beginning of personal isolation, which if not curtailed may result in behavior in the adult developing a superficial attitude toward others. Mature manipulation and disinterest in others may appear other than it actually is while providing for positive feedback for that attitude as a protective detachment. The way that we deal with others from a view of self-superiority, through a growing self-elevation, may reinforce this focus on oneself which may be seen as confidence and generally those leadership qualities which when pressed by others appears to be seen as control under pressure. So-called maturity, a dependable and an ostensibly responsive nature, may hide the beginnings of a drive to ultimately and solely serve oneself exclusively. The various incidences of hegemony and greed among businessmen, politicians, unions, corporations and other ideologues of often poorly disguised self-interest may have resulted from being misled by their impenetrably fixed thoughts onto a path by which group insensitivity has conspired to dispensed with fairness and concern for others. The real issue is why we tend to stay on such a narrow path? Why do we not take a rational position and question our error ? It is possible that we have been so desensitized for so long that we see avoidance of others as the acceptable norm, but the answer may not be easy or pretty: It may be we cannot seem to find the reins to check our runaway selfish desires.

There are many ways in which self may inappropriately exert itself, but we hide behind the notoriety of those that are caught in legal and personal violations of trust. American society is so caught up in a personal world view that it is hard to imagine it will ever be able to see very far beyond the wants of publicized corruption which is detached and impersonal to our world. Any view of candidacy is based on what can be mined for self from lending political support. The better good, the broader good is sacrificed to the personal needs and the recognition demanded of society. Corporations have little desire to restrict their marketing practices to America when more profit may be seen internationally. Unions push for concessions from business beyond what corporations are willing to commit to the long term often resulting in legal attempts to cut off pensions and perks. Celebrities speak without real knowledge of the cure for a disease that they have wanting research into cures to be better funded and, in effect, saving their lives. The idea of public servant, today probably an inappropriate term, but nevertheless, an idea of service beyond one's own immediate needs and concerns, has been all but lost. There is no sacrifice today in public service which is in many cases more profitable for the top leadership than for those doing similar work in the private sector with government officials voting themselves the raises that the private sector cannot. The "servants" of the people too often make more money and have more freedom to do as they wish than those that pay their salaries. The overall effect is that we do not seem to have expectations for anyone to be more than a servant of their own needs. The individual, it would appear, has come into it's own and will not be denied even while disadvantaging others.

The history of the individualization of life has come a long way from its lowly beginnings in antiquity. From the time that the masses were to have the ability to read and write, those talents used in the workplace turned to expressions of self-views and the even mockery of others. When education allowed the individual to reach beyond the competencies required to do a days work, the self and personal associations became enchanted with self concerns often to the exclusion of much or any consideration of others. The very idea that one could write down one's very impressions of life and could reach far beyond the close-in world of self, started a revolution much of which has devolved into gilded ephemerality and individuals mirroring the seeming limitless innovations of what would become an unstoppable modernity marked by a blatant disregard for others. The postmodern individual took a looser look at self in that the justification for being as one wished required only personal permission and despite the fact that a broad acceptance of considerate mores might appear to conflict with an individual or personal set of values, all inconsistencies were allowed to co-mingle looking optimistically yet unrealistically to meaningful and mutually accepting authorities.

Modern Americans have been accused of solipsism, in a strict sense of the term there is doubt that anyone could carry out such isolationism, but this could only be seen as an influence growing marginally in reality, since few would argue that they are alone and the sole possessor of existence. No matter the selfishness practiced by an individual, the very act of selfishness requires a requisite nod to others. Yet there is a practical hint of such thinking in that one sees all consciousness as at least secondary to that of one's self, if comparable consciousness is even accorded to any other. Conceding the existence of self, if not in actuality of others' existence, at least not the existence of another with any real importance, has brought the term solipsism into more common usage to describe a more solitary existence which many modern Americans seem to prefer. Associations are merely physical requirements for attendance with or acknowledgement of a tentatively shared and reluctantly conceded mutually conscious experience. To find reasons for establishing associations may seem totally selfish today with little being asserted except nominal that there is in reality mutually relational involvement. As Descartes had to look beyond his senses to a self-defining consciousness, to accept that there was a world beyond him, so the modern finds the benefits of association to be justification enough for merely nodding to the importance of others. I am, therefore, I need the illusion of others becomes the neo-Cartesian motif. Alice looking over the huge chess board questioned whether the world she was seeing really existed. If this world existed, were people merely pawns in her world ? On her chessboard, Alice trivialized the position and authority of the king.

The self as a physicality is impossibly philosophical, but as true to the label as possible one would only claim sole consciousness. Although sole existence may not be impossible for a child, all reality speaks to an inability to maintain this position. It is developmentally regressive for such an influences to direct ones adult understanding against the inevitable entropic judgment wrought on the observable human body. The young and their old aficionados seem to want to keep the denial of age alive and thereby much of the related "wisdom" concerned with behavior. In effect the inner and the outer understanding of a discontinuity of body and mind works to negate any power of morality and may compromise issues of obvious epistemology. Others become, for all intents and purposes, necessary phantoms and the undiminished moderns alone with their beneficent delusional associations. Others also have no unity of mind and body, but for all practical purposes must be seen as mere living representations of advantage. This pattern of exerted advantage seems too often to have little gain associated with it. The desire to exceed becomes an unstoppable motivation. From big business to the homeless, the gaining of more than comfortably profitability becomes an ineluctable end in itself. Even beyond need or even reasonable want a Dickensian drive to have more ever pushes to abstracted meaning. The excess becomes necessity and opposes all that stands in the way. More than the physical world and its possessions, obscure goals seem to be more psychological than material at times. The carving out of place among the many becomes an existential imperative for self and perhaps one's immediate clan. Others are relegated to peripheral concern and as the wagons of one's principles are circled to prevent outside advances centralistic behavior within the defensive group justifies all exclusion of others. Exclusion may be couched in reasoned discrimination as a judicious reckoning of that which is undesirable for the betterment of the clan and, therefore, bad or wrong. Ultimate justification for all activity, often no more than imagined comes from the protection of the group as the ultimate responsibility for self and associates. Exposure to the outside becomes formal and even digital, while passing off exclusion as manifestly obvious, the real yet elusive truth is that procedurally all decisions consist in self-determination.

And if we determine our justification for attitude and actions based on ourselves then why do we have to bring others into the fray ? If we are the exclusive and originary authority for what we do and why we do it, then why does it seem that others provide the ammunition ?. For instance, "I would not do that, except that she did that." There is more involvement with others which seems to be able to direct our actions and thoughts. This is not an indication that we are doing what we want to do, but is the result of what others have done that prompts our actions. This not only speaks to our not having complete control over our thoughts and actions, but we are reactive and the reason for our action is outside of us and in others despite our exclusion of others in forming an impression of who we are. This is a prime indicator that we are not apart from the will and wishes of other people. To deny our actions based on the actions of others would be to deny that there is no way to escape others. We are not motivated and do not act based exclusively on our own will and determination. We are goaded, if for no other reason, to demonstrate that we are ever manipulated by others, and have no holistic determination of actions that arises exclusively out of the self. Struggling for identity our expression of impatience and negativity is due to the frustration of loss of ourselves among the nameless others.

We become in the end what others, to some extent, make us. Even in our denial we take from them what we would have and begrudge them for what we cannot. We see them as ultimately resistance to our every success and progress. What a sad world this becomes.

Chapter 5

Why do we not let others win ?

I am always amazed when trying to get into another lane of traffic that too often someone will speed up to prevent my entry into their lane. Perhaps someone was late for work; this could explain the determined attitude, or perhaps my turn signal was not seen. These are definitely possible explanations, yet something tells me I am being to generous with explanations. I see this attitude, more often and excuses aside, as an instinctive response. A startling event comes to mind. I believe from the following example we may learn from the animal kingdom. A friend of mine had a gerbil which loved to get into a clear plastic ball and roll around on the floor. I was always amazed that except when in the ball the gerbil seemed to have little demonstrable personality. But when in the ball, and as driver, the gerbil showed a new nature and became the master of its own destination. Zipping around on the floor, it found not only a way to inform the world of its presence beyond a mere wheel-running rodent who had few existential possibilities. It would work at developing floor speeds that would allow it to cross the floor and rise up on the area rug. It would pause to plot its course, repeat its run ups against a raised rug edge and eventually was able to get on the rug and move about freely. What freedom it had found ! The most interesting event witnessed in this gerbil's out-of-cage recreation was to be seen in the acting out of attitude when the cat was around. Rodents and felines are resolutely conflicted under most circumstances with the cat being the potential aggressor, but, when in the ball, the gerbil was able to find confidence of the attack mode. No longer ignoring the cat or moving to the far side of the cage to avert any lethal encounters, the gerbil was clearly defensively protected and able to launch its calculated attack. When in the plastic ball, all was different, the small aggressor rolled relentlessly toward the cat until the cat yielded to its rodent rage. Repeatedly rolling into the cat, the gerbil found its revenge. In the cage the gerbil was merely defensive toward any aggressive act of the cat, but when in the ball, a layer of anonymity beyond the essentially impenetrable plasticity of protection took over. *Incognito* the rodent sought revenge. Revenge for what ? It had never been eaten, maybe scared or threatened but it had found solace in its cage. It was alway able to rely on the safety in the cage. But the gerbil could not move freely beyond the safety of is barred sanctuary; in the plastic ball his rug rage could be released.

The car is a freeing enclosure of sorts. We rodent-humans may find protection in willful steel-attack wheel enclosures rolling at the cars on our streets. Like the gerbil we seem to gain a transparent anonymity which may allow us to attain a faceless automotive emblem of selfish attitudes usually not acted on in our pure pedestrian form. On our own power out of our automotive armor we may appear less competitive and more controlled.

We want to win the race of cars, as we want to win in relationships which become competitions. In a marriage an undaunted will to exceed may drives one to become an attitudinal aggressor void of love and care for the other. I have never seen a divorce that did not come down to one or both sides wanting the most they could get first from the marriage then from the divorce. Although finding for your side against a spouse may be more easily accomplished, if for no other reason than emotional proximity, an objectification of relationships happens for some people at many personal and professional levels.

Have we turned our relationships into a super bowl frenzy, feeding on the fight for advantage and rolling over others to will an ultimate win for certainly Americans are enamored of such games and may give their free time to its pursuit perhaps with the idea that this is an attitude which best suits: one of adversarial and aggressive relations with others. Out of fear that we will be caged in a defensive posture or some sense that we are not up to co-existentialist survival, we may become the gerbil, aggressive beyond protective, reaching for our own purpose to the disadvantage of others we do not know and assuming that all others are cats. Restructuring our habits could help remove this drive to win. Not that I believe that only changing action will change attitude, yet it is a start.

The real issue is and the place to start is no more than the self-identity by which we navigate our lives. Our growth is attitudinal maturity, regardless of our age, subject to our understanding of ourselves beyond our physiognomy or success or failure. We are developmentally challenged by a world that changes and a persona that in response to that world may change. Shifting sands, fads and fashion, find no confident foothold. We see no immediate outcome of our energies or our sloth.

The world which is impossible to understand once and for all is no more an issue than that great non-understanding of ourselves which in persistent variance finds us to be fragile and vulnerable. We are in competition with others but often more by the environment of innovative flux in which we see our lives being tacitly measured. We text instead of talk, we dress for fashion and not for comfort or we dress for the ubiquity of events so as to make a blank statement of who we are and how we see all gatherings of people. We dress the same for the beach as we do for the job, school or church. Maintaining the same outward facade and the same inner protectionism we steel ourselves against a challenge to be vulnerable to comment or consideration.

Our cynicism pronounces our defensive strategies for personal survival. We are made secure in our aggressive and defensive modes. By keeping others out of our lives by such strategies we protect and pursue our lives in the surety that we will be, if not obvious winners in the competitive race for recognition and acceptance, at least not as losers. We look on excess and success as a threat to who we are and even our potential to see ourselves as, if not successful someday, at least not as abject failures in our own eyes.

In some distorted way we may consider being a respected human being means exceeding others in common easily recognizable goals and these are almost always based on exteriority and superficiality. What constitutes disrespect and seeking personal advantage over others may be seen as palpably in road rage as we undress others in face to face tirades. We become smaller when we keep others from being recognized by ourselves or others as less than worthy of respect or common communal courtesy. Although an attitude of solipsism is hard to imagine in reality, the autotelic nature of modern attitudes, that is personal behavior that finds a *telos* or end in oneself, is self-destructive as well as damaging to others. To encourage one to totally deny oneself is only considered of saints. Most of us are far from being considered for canonization, but but rather than finding an autotelic answer to our lives we must find in some if only small part of our lives a conscious heterotelic behavior, finding purpose in others apart from our needs. There is no reason in a balanced life for not letting others win. If for no other reason this helps us find more fully who each of us are.

Chapter 6

What do we stand to take from others ?

We may take from those we ignore or demean either by word or by neglect discounting usefulness and leaving them more apathetic to others. The way we interact with others may rob them of the enthusiasm and optimism about the world and their prospects in it. We may take hope that there may be a better life, good prospects for livelihood and liveliness, and by lack of concern and attention we may signal a feeling of less worthiness for others. Going forward, a person must have a sense of self-respect in order to take a serious responsibility for life and the life of others. To lose one's sense of self in full measure is to potentially alter the view one has of humanity in general. There seems no reason to believe that one who is untouched by the needs and hand of humanity can recognize one's own kind beyond their own position in life. Abuse very often produces abuse. One must not lose a desire to have an active membership within the human community. To see others as impositions or to disregard them is the beginning of a broader loss of human commonalities and a blatant disregard for their humanity.

Perhaps to view others as obstacles to our own success would support this disregard. Others may get in the way of our hopes and aspirations, success is limited, it would appear, but it is true that everyone wants control over their lives as much as can be managed. Why let anyone interfere with our chance ? We all want effectiveness in our daily lives. In a recent television commercial a woman claimed that she felt more in control of her life because of the extended functions of her phone. She seemed to have felt vulnerable without the critical phone functions she was advertising. Having a complete phone service, we are to believe from the commercial, made the young lady feel safe. Without special apps and functions, we are to believe she was not satisfied with her life. But with a full quiver of apps, she felt as if she had more "power."

If there is any truth in this television ad, are we to assume that the innovations of the external world are important to the image we have of ourselves. It is not hard to believe that, if reduced phone services can shrink our image of ourselves by the power we fail to wield, that other external factors may also affect our view of ourselves and others. I wonder if we can take a sense of not only power away from others, but, by our attitude and actions toward others, even substantial identity. In a race to see who can gain the most powerful identity we may almost fancy ourselves aspiring to the status of superhuman, the Nietzschean *Übermensch*. This does not mean super humane.

In our exuberance to become better in our own eyes, we may intervene in the lives of others to co-opt responsibility, or take over bailiwicks, leaving others less useful in their and other eyes. We, in our takeover bid, not only threaten to compromise a sense of self of another but may also reduce their enthusiasm and optimism about the world and their place in it. As all aspects of our lives are more or less intertwined we may leave another with less hope of better life, livelihood and liveliness. One's expectations must then necessarily be lowered and ultimately ones self-respect. This might be the result of our wanting to raise our own expectations and the respect that others hold for us in their eyes.

The larger question of our responsibility to others falls squarely on acknowledging and acting on the

recognition that others are as we, human. We are all members of a human
family. We stand to take that membership or reduce it to belonging to a subspecies of similarity, thus denying that we had similar beginnings and were to be looked on as equals, according to, if nothing else, our developmental sameness, both biological and psychological. From both effects we are likewise impressed with determinacy that is share by all of our kind. Some have more non-biological support than others but this cannot be seen as their being a qualified difference, only a disparity of advantages. If we acknowledge these physical and emotional exactitudes, we must, therefore, realize that we have absolute interests in others. To do less is to take away the very character that makes us human: extensive nurture, civility and awarding self-esteem without judgment. To do less is to relegate others of our own kind to a taxonomic inferiority. Ontological justification can be found for this only apart from reason. And in reality, taking dignity from others, that which we all should mutually enjoy, is only to take away virtue from mankind. By doing so we promote the same disjunction of innate interest, which in turn may be used by those which whom we have severed ties, and which will be passed along in unending debasement. In a more communal sense we stand to take from others the very thing we owe by kind, that is ourselves in support.

Chapter 7

What do we stand to lose of ourselves ?

Isolation for almost everyone proves over time to be devastating to hope and self-esteem. Some may seek solitude from fear or shame, others as a fortress from which not to hide but from which to strike out at others, the behavior seen from the Unabomber, Ted Kaczynski. Although highly intelligent, Kaczynski, pulled away from people to carry out a mission that involved the taking of human life. It would be hard to imagine that this isolationist behavior was the first evidence of pathological tendencies. The rejection of others as worthy of valuable acknowledgement had to precede such a horrific reign of terror.

In taking the lives of others Kaczynski denied the very identity of others in the human family, the very right of self-direction and even life with others. Although an irreversible effect resulting in death, his actions were a denial first of a patent disregard for life with others of his choosing, before the first victim died. The collective right that has emerged despite the tendency of despots to deny freedoms is irresistibly that of shared governance. Groups find associations through which an interdependent framework of trust arises and size and complexity result in the evolution. In an attempt to retain the original framework of organization a larger hope for integrity of purpose emerges. Down the way from originary motives we may lose the vision, and we may become lost in the envy of layered abilities and privileges. We look to others in this way with a lock on our position, not considering that, if we are not appreciated, we probably should move to a job for which we may find greater recognition of opportunity, but instead carp and darken the communications within sphere of influence allowed in the present job. Who loses in this situation ? Integral identity is lost failing to find right direction and instead resorting to sniping and compromising any good communications among those for which we have not found venom. Life with others, in the broader sense, is compromised.

So in what way do we compromise ourselves as we denigrate other ? There may be a belief that we are merely gaining an edge by self promotion. We may even become optimistic about the coupe which may aid us in our behalf, but in reality we are no more than taking a cynical view of others for our self promotion. The image that we conjure of ourselves distancing others as we move ahead is flawed for we are destroying the one thing that our self promotion cannot give - that is   trust. How can anyone view us as dependable and worthy of trust if we are capable of finding our advancement at the cost of someone losing their sense of self-esteem, one who has been denied worth by our actions ?

Within the group there must be some bond that goes seriously deeper than mere mutual service. It must come close to what one might find in familial contact: a sense of love. Not romantic love, as such, but love of   mutual involvement in something for which all are equally committed. There must be a sense of reasoned joy and love that transcends the aspirations of only one person. What we stand to lose is the augmentation of our efforts in denying others their rightful contribution to usefulness.

Chapter 8

How do we reclaim care in ourselves for the good of the lost others ?

We must first acknowledge that there are equally valuable lives all around us. That those that we know and that we don't know are worthy of having our attention and concern. Our differences should not be a reason for asserting our superiority. We must look beyond what we want and need for ourselves. Sacrificing to the greater good is what is only right: politeness out of a sense of others having value in themselves: to communicate without discriminating and when in association with others push for progress in relations, even friendship. We must open up a dialog of careful words and draw close to those commonalities that bind us one to another. To reach out to others not for our advantage but for what may be in time a growth of friendship or just a smile that could be accepted for genuineness of motives. Others are doing the very things which we should be doing. They are loving those close to them and holding out hope for their health and happiness, a wish for a long and prosperous life.

The first step back is to look beyond what we immediately want or think that we need.We must find a damper for our extreme materialism possibly by channeling our interests into an investment larger than our own: community, church, school, etc. We must practice charity and charitable thought, to put others in the picture. The result will be that to actually see others in their real lives not abstracted from a confrontational   automotive encounter or in isolated projection as the gerbil in the ball, will allow one to interact with others one on one with all the barriers removed. Sacrificing to the greater good, on our way back to civility, must necessarily begin with personal involvement not overlooking the circumstance of another nor seemingly fain an encounter with a measure of aloofness and distant politeness. We must step outside of our selves and lives and look for the inherent worth, the incalculable value in another. Face to face we cannot avoid the blanket incriminations and discriminations that boost us above others. Like friendship, practicing inter-relational exploration must be without condescension and with no expectation of gaining personal advantage. The dialog with which relationships are built will bring two possibly very different people together for unearthing and developing shared commonalities.

Returning to the fold must be the daily practice of openness and sharing. Do we avoid the person coming out of the grocery, or do we greet them and thank them for holding the door for us ? Do we hold the door for them ? Action is the only measure of our attempt to join common bonds with another. The idea that only those that are below us in station are to be seen as needy is condescending and misses the correct understanding of need. Like the monkey that was said to die when denied the comfort and warmth of a mother or a surrogate, society and community die without practiced concern, that is, looking beyond ourselves and our interests to the circumstance of others despite any superficial judgment that they have no real need of our attentions. We must convince ourselves of the truth: we are all needy and to deny that truth is to find ourselves withdrawn into a narrow world of narcissistic meaning and cut off from a world of individuals and groups that need others to merely exist is to deny, at our core, the need that one should have for another.

We must force ourselves out of solipsistic tendencies and reach out to others. Some may want to help in a soup kitchen, but why avoid those that in the normal routine of daily life pass by us unacknowledged. Open a door for someone or thank someone for opening a door, this requires only seconds of your time. Commit to a time in commitment to others in friendly concern and exchange at the expense of your own immediate interests. Change your schedule to interact with others by bypassing some of your own personal plans.

The road back must be laid with a foundation of hard resolve and paved with the determined openness to self denial and even acknowledgement of self deprecation. Acknowledge the very real possibility that you can and might be wrong. Let the other person win occasionally: certainly a large part of what we call love. For love rather than acceptance comes with the willingness to be inconvenienced and found wanting in understanding and action. Love may sound too strong a word for learning to get along with others, but can, when attention to others is given in ernest, be close to a proper understanding of a proper consideration of others. How else will a developed interest in others become a real dedication to others. Taking yourself out of you own concerns and replacing them for a time with the concerns of others would indicate that we find something in others more important that at least something of importance to us.

Chapter 9

How should we see the road back to others ?

'And has thou slain the Jabberwock?
Come to my arms, my beamish boy!
O frabjous day! Calloh! Callay!
He chortled in his joy.

We modern Americans spend our lives for ourselves in a sequence of micro-rebellions. In talk, traffic and even terror we see none but ourselves and give no concern but to who we are and our fate. This may seem harsh, yet in true confession would this not be found to be so ? How often during the day, any day, every day, do we think about the needs of others ? Television ads for charities may make us feel shame or relieved. We are not the ones in need, and so we are quickly pulled away to our own world of comfort. We soon wear off the guilt and become the centrist reason for existence among all the unthought needs of our world. Reason is suspended - we are in the world alone for all intents and purposes - yet, one would not want to the be the only person on the planet, left dwelling on the possibilities of solitude not by choice. Even in the compromise of solipsism, alienated from the family and friends, they may for a time have been our support until they offended. Then brother, son, wife all become anathema for we have created our world for ourselves alone. If others are willing to meet the challenging test of commitment, they may become new members of what could be a rapidly thinning cohort of hangers-on.

The enclave of mutual admirers may prove loyal to your cause, bow to your whims, even defend you against the ghosts which oppose you, still there is no room for more than minimal disagreement. This individualism is selfish yet requiring a paradox of loyalty whereby others are bound to the enclave by abstract dedication but the real and valued loyalists are those in the close circle of family and friends. Only in company of the self are the marginal members shown close-circle attention, but usually only when in attendance of the mock-community gathering. Those in such association are given importance and belonging and whether they are aware of the fragility of loyalty to them they may or may not even be known to the central figure. And the price of membership may prove far more personally expensive. The prime self thus gains the luxury of a following while the cabal is given little more than secondary consideration.

A change of attitude and true loyalty would begin the journey back to authentic concern for others once place and value for others is determined. Each of us should see the other person as potentially important, if not to us then to someone else which means that our responsibility is to enable that person to become what he or she can for others. We need to consider the feelings of others, even in the face of opposition and resentment. We need to apologize for our errors and make it known that this is not just a concession to form but is rooted in the best of all intentions. We need to let issues go, to forgive and not rehash the issues or pat ourselves on the back for having been so big as to allow another person to be forgiven. We must give the respect to others that we would wish to receive from others. The respect should issue out of an unmeasured consideration of what we could receive in return. A true understanding is in our ability to sacrifice for this change of attitude, to give even others the advantage of material benefit at our expense. Although this is not a wise measure necessarily for all issues of trust and concern for others, and, when in appropriately considered, such unwise relinquishing of hard judgment is potentially damaging to another's change of attitude toward those who would help. But one act of sacrificial care does not represent indisputable evidence of an attitudinal change. Care must be consistently and repeatedly offered to others even in the roil of personal attacks and accusations of condescension.

Don't expect this to spread like wild fire from one person to another. This is a difficult transition, and it will not necessarily find blanket acceptance for onlookers. Essentially the goal is to spread concern for others one person at a time. Even company ads on television are touting the line that we need to help others. No doubt there is inherent in the advertising that we have lost foundations of instinctual concern for others. We must march self-absorbed lifestyles back in order to recognize that we are not the only people on the planet and owe others basic respect and care. We must kill, or better allow the monster of self to die one giving gesture at a time.

So we may not receive praise from any other person for our efforts. Those that we befriend to help may not recognize our contribution to a better world as those around us who view our attitude as condescending to others, who most likely do not offer help to others. Realize that civility may cost the attention of others. How strange this would have sounded to Americans several decades ago. To imagine that helping others might be seen as some misplaced penance for an abnormal guilt or internal struggle with self. There will be those that view gentility and civility as a symptom of weakness. Those will merely vanish from your presence not wanting to stand with the strong.

Chapter 10

What would a true society of others look like ?

Concern and care for others is not without frustration. Alice's had her feet stepped on while the Mock Turtle and the Gryphon danced the Lobster Quadrille. Life with others will not be without its problems. But common goals can cement alliances.

Society is institutional and given by the acceptance of the majority purpose, divided by approach and moved forward by agreement to activity. What if everyone wanted the best for all ? From driving one's car according to government licensing and operational rules, for the good of the whole, to greeting everyone with a smile as they pass in close proximity. In a true society should not I see the other as my sister or brother Can the pressure of those who would have not concern for others rule our minds? How are we so different from others in our feelings and our aspirations for self-recognition? The same flesh, the same physiology and anatomy, roughly the same earthly desires - these are the solidifying commonalities of the species. My brother, if he is actively doing what is required to be my brother, respecting my right to partake of life considerately and freely, then a mutual working freedom becomes important to me. My needs are my brothers needs; my needs are my sister's needs. Linking my success to my sister's success binds me to another in present and future expectation, and I should be willing to relinquish my authority knowing that in doing so, my brother will represent me responsibly in any and all decisions.

Being linked with an-other means that the protection wished for is shared. When someone attacks my brother, that attack is also against my secure position. The idea of just war is founded on my being willing to give my life for my sister or my brother to protect either without being blinded to a secondary consideration that others may be finding illicit benefit in our concern. We must give to our brothers and sisters, however defined: those next door, those beyond our borders. Giving the ultimate sacrifice, to lay down my life for an-other knowing that in my death is a chance, if only a chance, for the survival of my more immediate kin or a more distant but brotherly human, is to value those above myself, an idea that seems almost fantastical to many today as a challenge to reasonable judgment. How would this change the way we might see ourselves and the world around us. Letting my concern for practical reason: my safety, my property and my self-esteem, become the reason for our defense of others is a decision that cannot be made using cold, analytical methodology, however, individual decisions given emotive reason will leaves us conflicted and can never tell us of our protective responsibilities to others in times of great or ultimate sacrifice. It is easy to say that we would not give that ultimate sacrifice, but we must see those in our protected past as either mad or suicidal. But to see them as caring for others human beings must give us a new perspective on mutual responsibility, if we have the ability to empathetically feel as we are by species so capable.

How different we see democracy and freedom today. Being benefitted by open pursuit of one's life, unfettered and unapologetic, such prodigality has become the measure of the blessing of personal authority. It has been tainted by greed and the chance to succeed at the expense of others. Today we are encouraged to do only what we want. The idea of a life of service to others is the reasoned and believed exclusive purview of any true understanding of missionaries and priests. Even the healing arts are seen as only profitable for financial success and less if at all for the responsibility that the medical profession should have for those sick or with infirmity. Some have seen the downgrading of lifestyle in medicine as a reason to go straight to the money in business and finance. The making of money for the shear profit of making money has drawn more to the bright future of guessing how money moves around in a sort of casino wager of economic and business pressures. This would not be the case if all viewed the needs and expectations of others with careful regard. But having taken the hands out of the work, investment is merely an attempt at controlling work without actually doing it and often with someone else's money. The idea of a civil servant is oxymoronic today. The term government employees more often brings to mind anything but not a servant of the peoples' needs. When government only spends money it does not make, and usually in extremely large bundles, it has not a sense of need for its provision and distribution. The size of expenditures cannot be understood in a one-to-one dispersal of funds. The idealism of laws and bills that allow massive allotments of money is seen in the unavoidable abstract nature of legislation. We have not only lost the ability to see the needs of others, but without that personal recognition of need we have lost what a government of, by and for the people must look like. We cannot see beyond the distally organized government offices to each person, if we cannot acknowledge each person we pass for their right to respect, concern and help if needed.

Today the idea of helping someone else in need is better seen as a government obligation or professionally related task. When we look at the eleemosynary provision of personal grants in aid, we become suspicious and smell scams. In a true society that felt the pain of a sister or brother there would be no need to be cynically disposed to giving to an-other's need. We would lose some of our practical wisdom to the chance that someone had a pressing need which could be eased by our attention and concern. We would stand to be taken advantage of in that we would hope that any need we might have would be met with the same concern and trust in the validity of the need. Our willingness to step out of our own concerns to service an-other's need is the mark of a true citizen and collectively a true society, and the claiming of a good nation and a great nation.

Our very purpose, as individuals and as a nation, arise from the recognition that the world outside of ourselves is dependent on our involvement, yes, even serious consideration of the other person. Few spend the bulk of their day alone carrying out the schemes of solitude. The plenary nature of society is based on the integral activities of those at least marginal members that reach out to find meaningful work and contractual agreement. Most such interactions are not the result of hostile takeovers but require a coordinated concession to one another. The digital and business age in which we live has given us examples of a more aggressive approach and less caring communication with work and purpose. Certainly the cellular age has made interaction a mechanical and even linguistically limiting experience. I was struck by the preferable facility, even the insular advantage, of the the cell phone, when a friend was driving his two daughters, one in the front seat and one in the back seat, and they were carrying on a digital conversation as they were communicating vocally with others in the car. When communication takes on the title of multi-tasking, it begs the question - was any of the information past between parties in that car considered important from either a knowledge or relational perspective and any oral conversation was diminished by the lack of focused attention given to the words of others.

Whatever a true society would appear to be it must be based on the assumption that others are not only important but deserve our concentrated and undivided consideration in all matters. To see ourselves as society members asking that all authority be given to us is not only patently selfish but is contrary to the working concept of community and nationhood on which we have drawn liberally for so long. Society should be a mutual understanding and practice of concern for others. It should not be marked by draconian pressures to require all citizens become interactive members to promote some abstract beneficial group purpose. Nor should individualist tendencies be given the authority to justify separatism in response to personally rejected group purpose. Those that are thus guarded must step outside of any counter-productivity by which walls of separation are erected and self aggrandizement is given the ultimate value. Without compromising beliefs or denigrating principles, all should become advocates of the society in which they live and thrive. Society starts with the help and good wishes of every one of our citizens who give of who they are without expecting a return.

Conclusion

Thumbing one's nose at authority is done everyday by most of us. We decide not to recognize the speed limits, we find loop holes on our tax form and we commit to business as if it were a crime for which we might profit and for which we will most likely not be arrested. We become the product of an attitude not totally of our making but stand behind its arrogance as if it were our idea completely. We often build our communication around the language and disposition of wags. A selfish and greedy attitude is our lot unless we are able to return to a respectful neo-communitarian life which would correctly balance the individual's interests with that of the good of all. When the darker attitudes of self push back the needs of others, then others are taken advantage of. That great comedic movie and social commentary entitled *Groundhog Day*, depicts a man locked in the repetition of a single day in his life, the same day over and over. The opportunities become obvious early on. The first inclination is to take advantage of the situation, since no one else knows that he is revisiting each day as the same day with knowledge of the same-day events. Everyone else is only experiencing that day once. Phil decides first to do what ever he wants to take care of himself and to use anyone else as he wishes. Since he knows all that will happen in the curse of the same day, a day in which he is trapped, he has, what would appear to be eternity to plan and scheme to his own ends. Yet after some time, if you can say that about the recurring same day, he finds that he is in the throes of despair and attempts killing himself time and time again. Even this attempt to end it all fails to stop the repetition of the same day. Each day, the same day, he rises to the same radio-alarm clock program with the same music and commentary. Eventually he is returned to real time, a return to a day-at-a-time sort of existence, but not before his having realized that to live in that one day forever must bring more than self-gratification, or if he had to live that one day ending it all would not only not be possible but would waste the time to help others who only saw one day as their loss and his end. Gaining the upper hand does not sustain lasting value for him. By the end of the movie he has becomes quite helpful, grown to appreciate higher-minded disciplines and come to be highly valued to all around him.

What a moral, if only we could learn from Phil. Doing only what we want and striving for self-satisfaction can only lead to a sad and joyless life. We have been sold a lie. The lie is that we can find happiness by serving only our needs and our wants. I do not know that we moderns can find a way back to the others, but, without the turn taken by Phil in the movie, we do not have a collective future as a society. With a return to real time and events, Phil took time to consider others in his life and found the value in each new day for himself and for others. Like Alice we can step back through the mirror into a concerned world of communities. Phil's lesson was that ultimate control of one's life without others may be protracted time but not necessarily protracted happiness. Life is fulfilled as we becomes servers of others. The most rewarding world can be found as we step back through the mirror and into a world of people, civil associations and more responsible and kinder behaviors.

Time and timing are the keys to turning around the attitudes that will usher in cordiality. The culture of insensitivity is at work everyday to influence all that are susceptible to cynicism and disrespect. Attitudinal sloth has filtered into our lives by the influence of entertainment modeling getting what we want and the inability by practice or by ignorance to see the value of others. Such behavior and attitude would once have been thought too crude to exact laughter in all but the hard and sociopathic. Today most find the dark societal humor acceptable and even choice entertainment. The effect has been that we tend to value little and desire more for ourselves. This is a cycle of discontent and unending disappointment. The way back must be a calculated move. Defamation has plagued groups who have later turned the tables on oppression and cynicism and taken a stand for emotional repatriation demanding respect and equality. We must begin to stage morality lessons: how one should behave around and toward others. Perhaps a larger PR campaign must be undertaken to bring a country of individuals bent on their own agendas to give proper valuation of others.

We are now living a Hobbesian nightmare. The loss of others is the loss of respect, order, humanity, trust, friendship and community. A valiant effort should be begun to establish an alliance among citizen, that recognizes the needs of others, not on a charitable basis although this has been lost also, but on grounds of a return to civility and concern, to begin to relearn as a nation how to forgive and accept those around us as the same, those just like ourselves. To give ourselves to others sacrificially will make them appear important to us and they may even smile on us.